AF323950

— *no mind* —
right hand in the left hand
like a bird

Also by Thomas and Karen Fitzsimmons

Is Two :: Becomes One
Build Me Ruins
Iron harp
Fencing the Sky
Zia
Water Ground Stone
Rune of Stone
A Green and Golden Bird
The Great Hawaiian Conquest
The 9 Seas and the 8 Mountains

High Desert //

// High Country

Seeds

Sumi Paintings :: *Karen Fitzimmons*
Poems :: *Thomas Fitzsimmons*

KATYDID BOOKS
Santa Fe
2007

KATYDID BOOKS

#1 Balsa Rd., Santa Fe, New Mexico 87508
sframbler@gmail.com

ISBN 978 0-942668-67-4

Produced in the United States of America by
KT DID Productions.

First edition

Thank you again, Pieter.

Contents

skeleton trees reach
into a wild northwest gale
twist it into song

High Desert High Country

Badlands

miles away dawn paints
the ice peaks crimson   here one
soaring red-tailed hawk

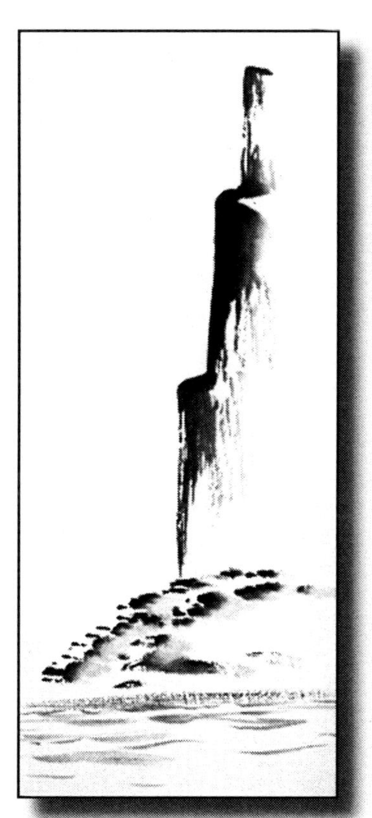

sun holds hard to this
high desert where a once great sea
came to rest and died

on these ridges
wind harvests the ultimate form
dust

clouds from two oceans
hang dry over bare arroyos
rabbits mad with thirst

*setting sun hangs
in a twisted web of Rio Grande
winter trees*

*steep arroyo walls
held by   holding   cactus root
rock-veins   rattlesnakes*

sunset — crimson buttes
ignite in a turquoise sky
explode in the mind

surging orange clouds
slide the sun's radiance
into night's long cave

carmine cactus cups
reefs of blue asters   new
coral of a now dry sea

snow on desert stones
builds up minarets and domes
no camels   no prayers

two raw-boned mustangs
one still standing   one down
vultures hang in the sky

in the arroyo
one bright-chested flicker
one rusted pickup

Pueblos

bare winter vines
all muscle and sinew
the Old Ones laugh

cock calls the dawn
down through thunder
time changes color

snow drives through
broken pueblo walls   buries
the silent kivas

firelight trance
and chant spill them out into
now and they dance

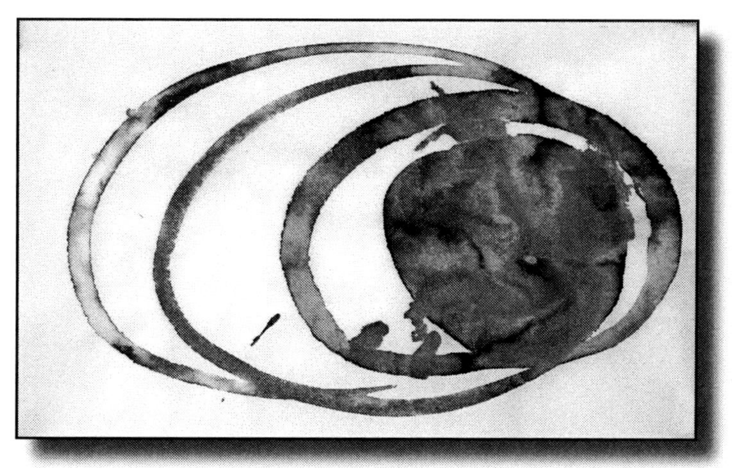

in pueblo ovens
new bread swells with drumbeat
prayer   song

pueblo Indians
hymn their borrowed Christian saints
dance the corn   the deer

from the circle
foot-beat   song   & pollen rise
to greet the eagle

low clouds swirling snow
fold into evening silence
ghosts in the fire

Spanish Holy Names
hide the broken skulls and bones
under pueblo churches

'round Quarai's mute red
ruins ghosts and cottonwoods
still rattle & dance

the old worn trails
lead to turquoise mines silent now
as the ruined kivas

ice on pueblo walls
frozen tears of those who once
sang here

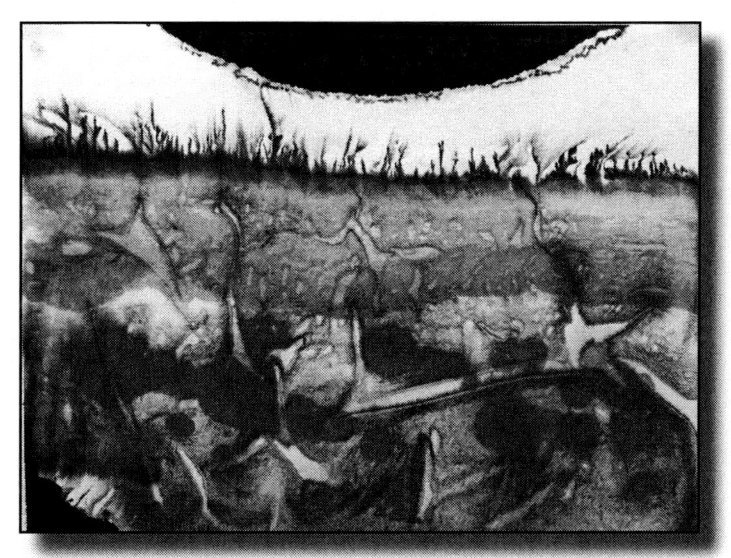

Rio Grande Country

*Rio Grande slips
along burnt buttes and mesas
only this water*

— dawn —
mind is a red
pine

Rio Grande cuts through
highway rubble as the big trucks
bust the road above

seen in the shrinking
river the old cottonwoods
die twice

tree dome over river's
spring surge shelters young swallows
from hawk   eagle

currents swirl
eight ways at once   eagle
still grabs his fish

rockwater bubbles
dance unbroken on one fixed point
by a shattered boat

from a craggy black
rock in a snarl of white water
one small red bird fishes

Rio Grande's lode of
ghost gold stories still shimmers
in the gorge's dark veins

where white water roars
through redrock & pine jumble
the eagles slide and soar

new piñon pine
shelters under the juniper's
green dome

sacred Black Mesa
bang in the center of a
run of jade grassland

one dozen painters
one only mountain
one dozen mountains

Taos Mountain
no temples   no hermits
just there

Trails

slick rock trail
into a northwest gale
the simple life

ice cliffs shimmer
through dawn-feathered mist
time to climb

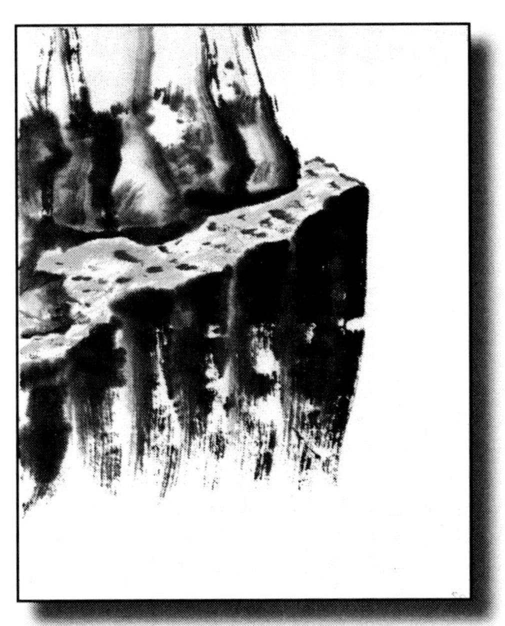

from iced rocks and roots
trail edge plunges straight down to
childhood terror

violet winter fog
shrouds the peak's long white
down-reaching claws

from banked trail side snow
icy fingers reach out for
eyes   throat   lungs

white clouds merge into
white snow   no edge no seam
we have been eaten

tight cliff-side trail
through blinding glare   no place
to look but in

red lace of fall grass
frozen into snow glows warm
beside the trail

footfall on snow–crust
blue jay shrieks a warning
through evening silence

lemon leaves on bent
aspens hold in a wind that
all but knocks us down

Village and Town

the old adobe church
folds the cold desert night
around its candles

snow melt surging down
the acequias   nudges spring
asleep in its seeds

in the hill cabins
only candlelight fills the red
clay wine cups

sunbeams play along
the strings of an ancient harp
the dust dances

blue sills and doors
in earth–brown adobe walls
are "gates to heaven"

redwing blackbirds speed
through alfalfa green by gold
the only traffic

of nine cows two are
heavy with calf   late morning
sun slips into the barn

coiled cat sleeps
while horses snort and stamp and
the barn dust goes gold

cottonwoods chatter
as Karen sketches me by a
cracked raw-weathered barn

wind flings page and pen
across hard-packed barnyard clay
poem toe dance

bent pickups angled
into roadside mud and stones
"Barb's Hair Styles"

orange hose   lemon suds
cricket on a lime green bucket
carwash

sunset brings
snow and sunbeam rhumba
tequila

in mountain villages
tin-roofed churches rusty gas-pumps
wildcats bears eagles

long white whiskers
slide through graveyard shadow
inquisitive cat

Mine Shaft Saloon
old guys hard guys in big black hats
beer from Belgium

standing on the corner
long legs   red boots   short skirt
keen wind

Essential Others

north slope ponderosas
shelter bears foxes snakes
essential others

Buffalo Mountain
foothills gathered close
as calves

grass   bush   tree
in dawn–lit frost
each its own ghost

dawn rangeland scroll
lavender snow   pink ice
purple cattle

coyote pups curled
cool in a culvert where red-hot
pavement leaps a ditch

pack horses lurching
out of deep valley drought
smell the upland streams

in this morning's rare
wet herb-scented desert air
the flycatchers feast

evening tide of
dolphins mustangs whales giraffes
floods the turquoise sky

this hard dry land feeds
spiders ants coyotes snakes
flowers beyond count

perched on Rowan tree's
pyramid of red seed-berries
one sunstruck robin

door slams   starving
coyote gulping green olives
tries to run   stumbles

hummingbird
swoops down on tall torch lilies
sunblaze in its wings

Great Horned Owl
hoots us back to our long ago
nights in caves   no fire

deer
dying in chest deep snow
poised

Apache Canyon

mountains
blue in dawn sky
fox cough

in the arroyo
sun strikes frosted cactus thorns
instant galaxy

wild grasses bowed
by winter gale and snow
spring to the new sun

on a tree rotting back
into black mud green slime
year's first yellow lark

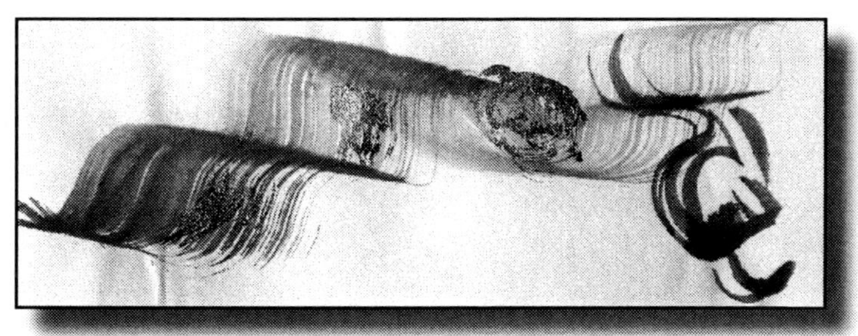

clouds gold into blue
flood the evening sky   nighthawk
calls in the stars

autumn birds
one last song and gone
the long white waiting

ravens and children
follow the deer dragged through snow
to knife   fire

gold grass   scarlet berries
burst up through violet snow
Christmas baubles & bells

last of the snow
sucked into towering pines
dwarf cactus

yellow moon
sails the long thin rivers
coyote prowls

walking by water
sun in one hand moon in the other
cross the stream

harvest moon
balanced
on a cactus stalk

crescent moon slips
through summer's spray of stars
coyote howls   loon laughs

Glorieta Mesa

buffalo grass   pepper sage
speckled trout in a cold fast creek
eagle takes a look

scent of snow and new
cut pine almost fills the air
vultures   one dead deer

cicada love songs
trill through twilight thunder's
dark hollow growl

new widow's garden
full of bluebirds bees and
big blossoming trees

thick old cedars
drink sunlight moonlight starlight
live long   long   longer

under a window thick
with ice an indoor fountain
ripples a watersong

rabbit poised by the road
pink nose twitching to cross
raven hovers

wild horses flare
through scarlet chaparral
clinging spiders

in a time drenched with
the stench of torn flesh fried blood
dawn gold on aspens

black ants swarm the trail
the early morning news
counts yesterday's dead

around each plant
a mound of sun-filled snow
heron and her young

the setting sun melts
mountains buttes & mesas to
just this cicada song

winter wind whispers
through the old cabin's logs
whose story

Home

breathe just right &
every cell flops over
grinning

orange violet green sky
scarlet almost purple mesas
home

elegant
under the silvery aspen
rattlesnake

sparking morning frost
green chile stew & coffee black
snow and sun tango

sun melts high–ridge snow
mountain bluebirds rim the water
two sons here at once

rainy evening
moon in the window
lemon dahlia

eros
two limbs of candle wax
straddle the flame

lazy twilight talk
cold pints of crisp pale ale
the desert's dry love song

wind howls and bangs
on the darkening window pane
one translucent lacewing

you paint I write
bluebirds flock   sing   leave
another year

sun splits a grey sky
I wake from a night of
dancing with old bones

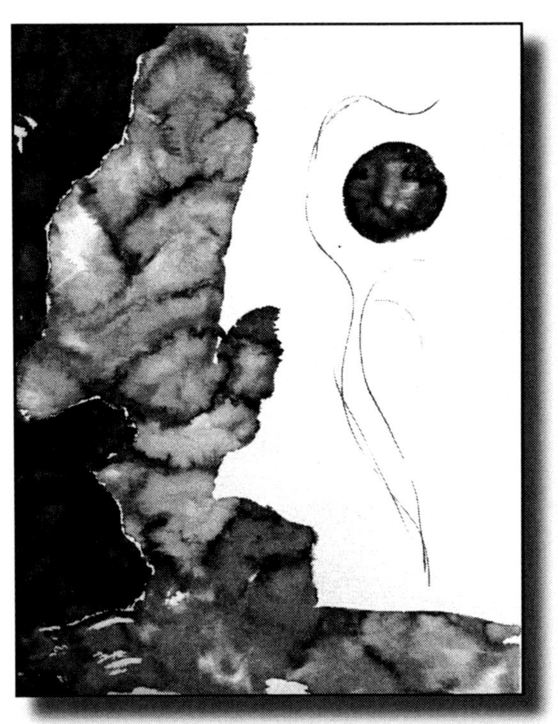

red rock mountain glow
breaks through morning pain
will I ever climb again

this year's finches
nest in the honeysuckle
horned owl just above

year's last snow melts
into dust and apple blossoms
mother   ninety   dies

at the water basin
bluejay and robin face off
mano a mano

silverlace vine
climbs our tall adobe wall
slow lightening

blue black clouds smother
the first bright gleam of dawn
the morning paper

millennium's end
ice holds the high passes
in a butcher's grip

sharp–needled cholla
offers up its purple blossoms
another friend dead

northwest gale slams at
the house howls down the chimney
my father's   my rages

within white clouds
tides of gold and silver
on my page   one line

between two ancient
junipers San Pedro's snow
cloaked peak hovers

through the window
a sweep of evening clouds
in the mind   quiet

neighbor puppy
left out all night long   screams
owl drops us his skull

owl on the roof names
all the long-ago shipmates
killed by moonlight

carmine leaves curl in
cold dawn light   by the window
a yellowing diary

shriveled apples
on a dry tree
these hands

hummingbird zooms in
to check the reds and golds
of my Spanish vest

honeysuckle scent
just barely there
everywhere

robins this winter
did not go south   stayed with
you and me and the dog

two haiku
on a pain free day
what next

dream ice on long pale
Chiricahua river stones
Geronimo's bones

at nightmare edge
boot tips just past the rim
why not

me
&
the mountain

the mountain
and
me

the
mountain

Her Garden

lightening & whirlwind
tear at the hunched black garden
just this martini

settled in at last
we wake to three coyotes
prowling the garden

on a bent cosmos
the goldfinch stands on its head
harvests new seed

in the spiked arms
of a thick cholla cactus
four purple finch eggs

first iris of the year
one yellow one magenta
dancing arms   small faces

night sucks light
out of clouds ridges hills birds
the roses go last

rustle and scurry of
something tiny in the grass
nighthawk flashes in

the gay plum dwarfed
by a massive olive tree
another war

grazing jackrabbit
hard to shoot when the sun shines
through his ears

by scarlet flax
blazing in high-desert air
blue flax whispers water

evening grossbeak
bathes in the new morning sun
time turned upside down

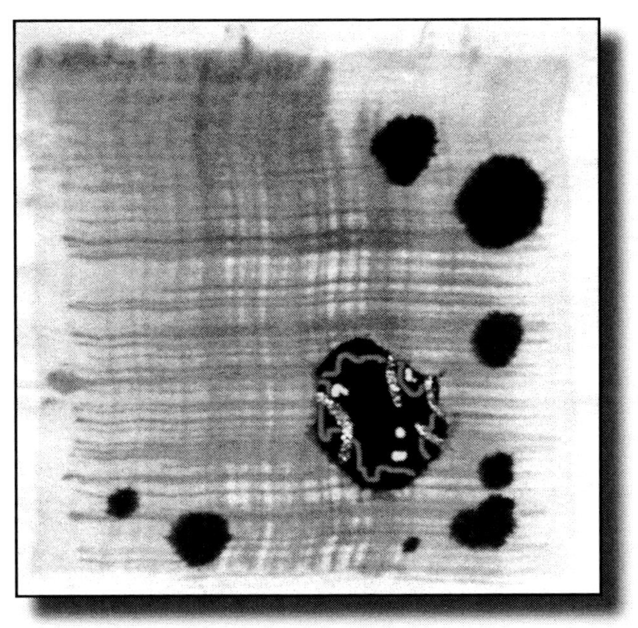

elves & dragons race
through an endless curve of sky
in our garden   gophers

sun-crusted desert herbs
monsoon pops the seals
we reel

finch in the wind
snatches seed from a rocking
rolling dahlia

crimson swarms along
black aphid-covered branches
lady-bugs   too late

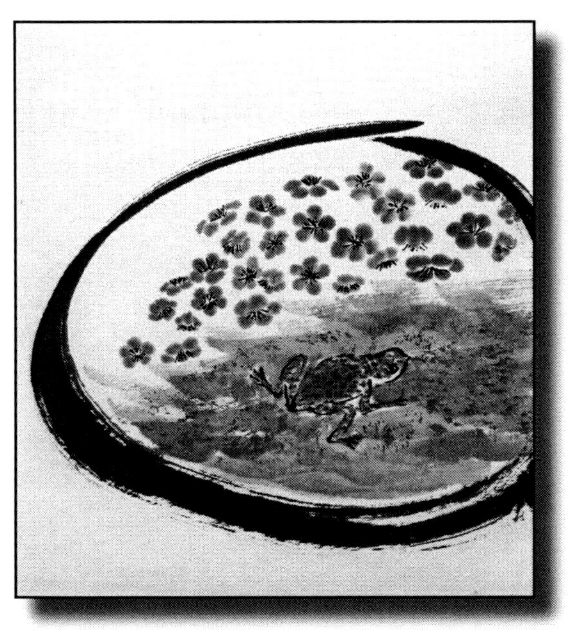

in the dazzle shade
of pink and white apple blossoms
a wary horned-toad

— iris —
early morning light
twist

jay feeds his mate
sitting squawking on the eggs
domestic blues

here come the quail
strutting their Sunday best
hats purses and all the kids

robin gathers strips
of loose honeysuckle bark
new nest

white stones in a black
basin   two bluebirds bathe
*   two ravens argue*

a dozen eager quail
at our stone water-trough
hawk shadow — gone

in the scorched garden
a green rock from a far lake
the one sign of water

lightning flashes
through swift rolling black clouds
in the garden   fireflies

flat white river stone
on a curved black marble slab
full moon at dawn

moon–leached clouds over
sleeping Jemez volcano — here
a sloughed-off snake skin

the rowan tree's red
late-summer berries erupt into
autumn-wind polka

last golden apples
on the bare Indian Magic
hold the dawn's song

late fall roses
flow summer's fire deep
into evening cool

October gale
tosses branches and birds   we reap
blossoms and feathers

meadowlark lands
on a snow–capped juniper
sun crystal fountain

trees & bushes gay
in bright capes white hats
Easter snow

dry roses
hold their skeleton past
long into winter

sun on snow
the whole dawn jewel box again
foal's breath lingers

pear blossoms dance
in a veil of white wood-smoke
spring dawn tantra

pregnant rabbit dodges
insistent males as a nesting
blue jay arrows by

year's first butterfly
tours new garden freshness
gathers   sows

hummingbird feasts
on Jupiter's Beard blooms
god-food for a faerie

dry leaves curl carmine
on autumn Barberry bushes
raven squawks in the snow

Mars red in the east
blinks in Jupiter's white stare
we dream we are here

a glass of red wine
holds the Rose and the crimson
Sangre de Cristo peaks

Skelly

The Terrier

autumn to winter
deer flow down the mountain
terrier in my lap

I sit and sit
and try and try to meditate
Skelly sits   gazes

heavy grey morning
drifts towards the rocks
Skelly brings a toy

Skelly prances
behind his Buddha nose
always here and now

hears sees and smells it all
sleeps and sleeps
and sleeps

in early morning cool
newborn Jay hides in the vines
Skelly points just where

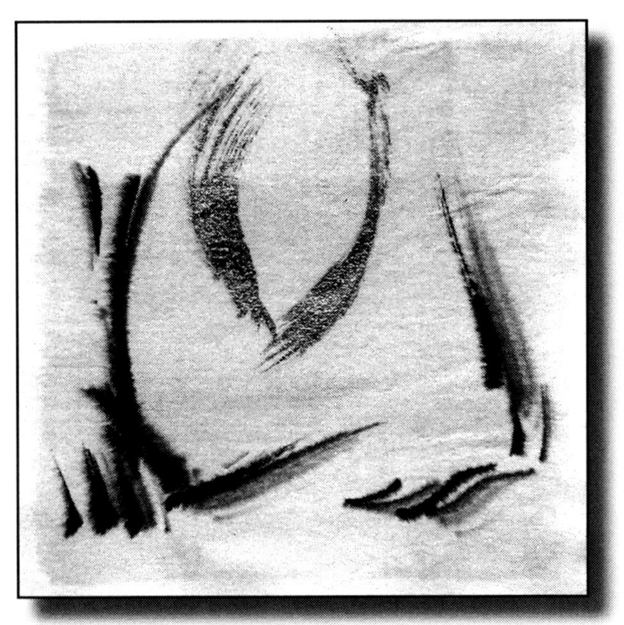

tall grasses all but
hide the rabbits ears
all but

Karen and Skelly
off for a walk   his legs blur
Karen hangs on

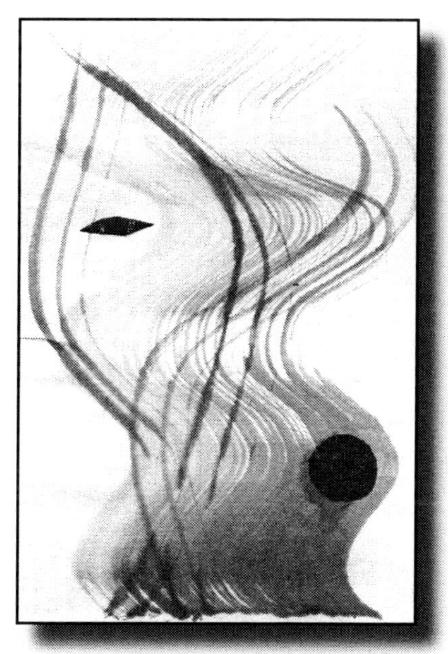

he reads the scroll
of a long high-desert trail
Buddha ears bouncing

at the old well we
stare far down at ourselves
up here   Skelly growls

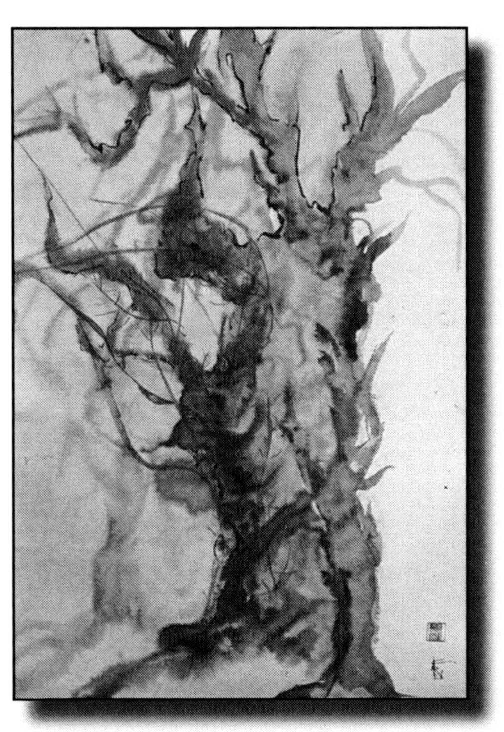

scent of sage and pine
mix of apple pear and peach
Skelly is bewitched

terrier at our feet
whiskey in our glasses
we sing down the sun

swims through nose-high snow
dives in   rolls   wriggles
grins

Skelly checks out the
garden after rain   shipmates
and a new port's bars

end of day brings news
of world–wide horrors   Skelly
watches the sunset

wags his tail
greets something we cannot see
in the wind

fir and aspen hills
the universe just beyond
us and Skelly here

Galisteo Basin

red fox hunkers
under new bluebird nest
waits

contrails ice the sky
meadow-larks streak through the high
spring grasses

Rowan trees bow
to a northwest gale   coyote
kneels at the stream

pounded by the sun
the dying cattle still circle
a warped dry water-tank

the bunkhouse keeps them
dry — cowhands cats lizards
roaches mice snakes

over rock and rut
a yellow butterfly holds fast
to the snorting pickup

birds falter
streams thicken and sour
we are here

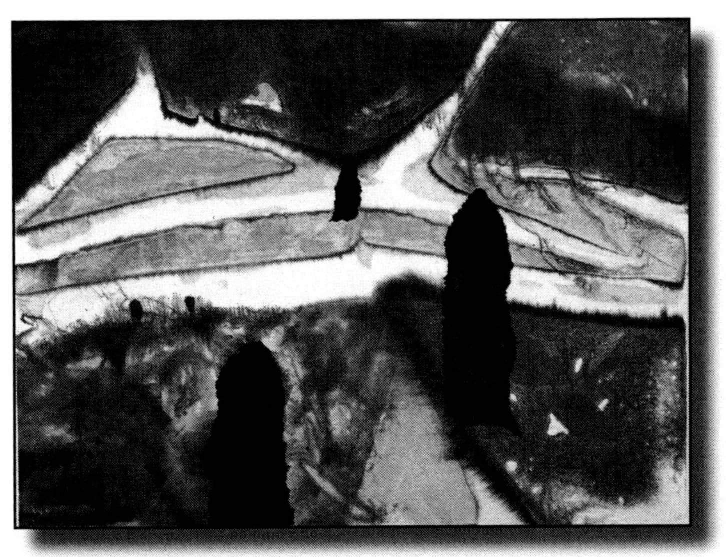

openers and benders
united against the left hand's
clumsy innocence

muscle car roar
force feeds
the blob at the wheel

one hand
always colder than the other
the killing hand

black stitching across
a savanna of drifting snow
barbed wire

in a bleached arroyo
a smear of orange water
pickup rusting

old adobe church
besieged by sunhats and easels
the ravens leave last

on the road early
bumping along burping
Route 66 bacon

from the rotting hut
a rusted bell leans into
bright mountain rain

without candles
night rules
some are candles

Mountains All Around

on the wind whipped ridge
a butterfly suns itself
in a bear track

Mesa Verde's
spirit sky-drum
hum

Valle Grande
copper grass dancing in
volcano's navel

death
is not other   what ends
begins

cedars black
into green blue dappled dawn
two herons rising

ponderosa pine
tall against north snow ridges
Basho's staff

night mountain fog
bites into my cheeks & eyes
cedar smoke

fallen cliff rocks bright
in fast green water   time flakes
in a liquid clock

two deer   one fawn
on eastern slope   small suns
wet on tall grasses

on the edge of water
the setting sun will lay a lick
of light straight to you

in volcano's mouth
cattle and coyote doze
road snarls by

above a rising roll
of snow ridges & massed pines
the single eagle floats

clouds flock around
the crimson Sangre de Cristo
herded by the sun

yellow and crimson
bloom out of black coal slag
on the ravaged slopes

red pines that cooled
Anasazi caves now shade
uranium streams

town bank and church
nestle below the old gold seams
of St. Peter's peak

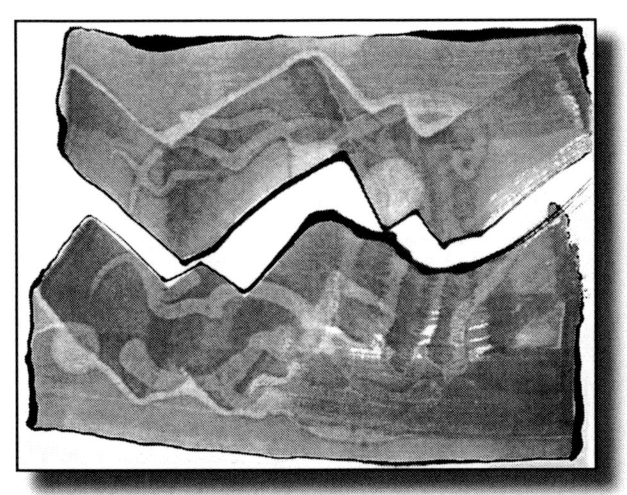

on Ortiz mountain
sagging miners' shacks once
tea now and boutiques

on a sodden mountain
first sun through dawn mist finds
three red poppies

burst of blue asters
just where the trail falls into
another black gorge

in the swollen stream
a newly free fallen leaf
flirts & dances

through a sullen sky
suddenly on the mountain

sun

ah
the sound of one's soul
clapping

Karen and Thomas have lived much of their lives in other countries, including 10 years on and off in Japan. In the mid-1970s they did a 16 month, 18 nation poetry-performance\lecturing\workshops tour through the Western Pacific, South Asia, the Middle East and Europe under the auspices of the United States Information Service (USIS) and the State Department. They have for 25 years published, for distribution by University of Hawai'i Press, a series of modern Japanese poets in translation (30 volumes), and another series that considers and reflects Japanese aesthetics.

While in Japan, Karen studied oriental brush painting with a Japanese master and now teaches it here. She also works in western modes — oil, watercolor, pastel, collage, monoprint. Thomas has written, translated, and edited a large number of books. They live just south of Santa Fe, New Mexico.